Middle School
Math Challenge

Written by Daniel W. Ary • Illustrated by Kelly Kennedy

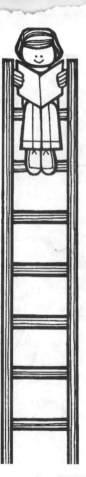

The Learning Works

Editing and typography by Kimberley A. Clark

Copyright © 1995
THE LEARNING WORKS, INC.
P.O. Box 6187
Santa Barbara, CA 93160
All rights reserved.

Printed in the United States of America.

ISBN: 0-88160-267-1

Introduction

Middle School Math Challenge is packed with lively and creative instant activities that can be used in a middle school classroom in a variety of ways:

- class openers
- "problem-of-the-day" challenges
- homework assignments

- extra credit
- classroom bees or contests
- supplements to topics covered in class

The format of this book makes it extremely flexible and easy to use. The activities can be reproduced and used with students in the ways listed above, or you can read story problems aloud as "brain-teasers" to get your students thinking.

Problems cover such curriculum areas as integers, fractions, division, multiplication, logic, probability, percentages, statistics, algebra, geometry, patterns, and number sequences.

Middle School Math Challenge provides middle school teachers with activities to motivate, inspire, and otherwise stretch middle school math students in lots of fun and creative ways!

CONTENTS

Contents
(continued)

Contents
(continued)

Only Primes 2, 3, 5, or 7

In this puzzle, three digits are provided as clues. Fill in the boxes below with the prime numbers 2, 3, 5, or 7 so that the multiplication makes sense.

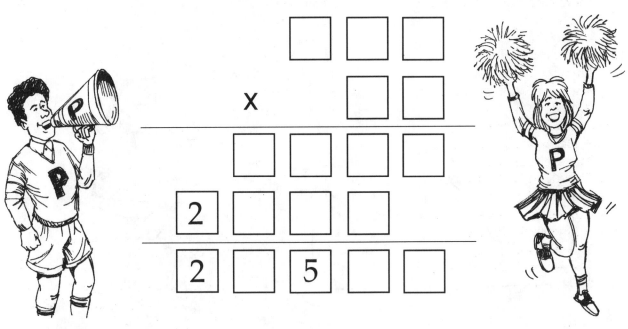

A Crystal Lattice

The lattice puzzle below is made of circles and lines. Each line joins three circles. Select different integers from 1 to 15 and fill the circles so that each row totals 20. Not all 15 integers will be used. One integer is used twice and has been filled in for you.

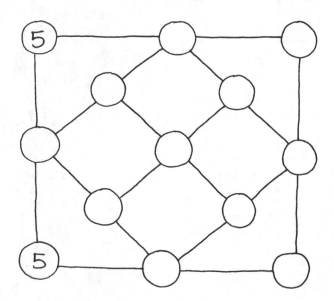

It's Raining! It's Pouring!

It was a dark and stormy night. As the clock struck midnight, it began raining cats and dogs. Will there be sunny weather in 96 hours? Explain why or why not.

Now That's Some Gas Mileage

Igor is a famous inventor. He has designed three fuel-saving intentions for cars. He boasts that his inventions will provide the following savings on fuel:

Invention 1: 35%

Invention 2: 40%

Invention 3: 25%

Igor claims that people can get 100% savings on their fuel by using all three inventions. Is this possible? What did he do wrong? How much savings could a person get if all three inventions worked as advertised and independently of each other?

My Family

I have as many brothers as sisters, but each of my sisters has only half as many sisters as brothers. How many brothers and sisters are there in my family?

Pig

Number of players: 3 to 4
Materials needed: a pair of dice

Each player begins with zero points. Player 1 roles the dice. If the dice come up anything but a pair, the total of the dice is added to the player's score. The player then has the choice to keep rolling and add to his or her score or to pass the dice to the next player. However, if the dice are thrown and a pair shows, the dice must be passed to the next player and all points made by the player during that turn are lost. If a pair of ones ("snake eyes") shows during any round, the player loses all the points gained up to that point in the game. The player who is the first to reach 200 points wins the game.

What Happened to the Extra Dollar?

After a late-night soccer game, three players were too tired to drive home. They decided to rent a motel room for $60.00 so they could get a good night's sleep. Each player paid $20.00. After they had gone to their room, the manager realized that he had overcharged them $5.00. He gave the bellboy $5.00 and told him to give the money back to the men. On the way to their room, the bellboy realized that the $5.00 could not be divided evenly among the three men. He decided to give each man one dollar back and keep $2.00 for himself.

At this point each man paid $20.00 and got $1.00 back. So they paid $19.00 each. If you multiply $19.00 times three people, you get $57.00. Add to this the $2.00 the bellboy kept, and you get a total of $59.00. What happened to the extra dollar?

A Bad Check

John went to a sports store to buy a tire pump for his bike. He selected a model that cost $15.00. When he got to the counter he realized that he had forgotten his wallet at home. He did, however, have a check for $25.00. John convinced the owner of the store to take the check. Not having the correct change, the owner went to the adjacent shop and exchanged the check for two tens and a five. The owner then kept $15.00 and gave John $10.00 in change. John left, never to be seen again. A few days later the check bounced. The owner of the sports store made the check good to the shop owner who took the check.

If the pump originally cost the sports store owner $9.00, how much money did he lose in the deal?

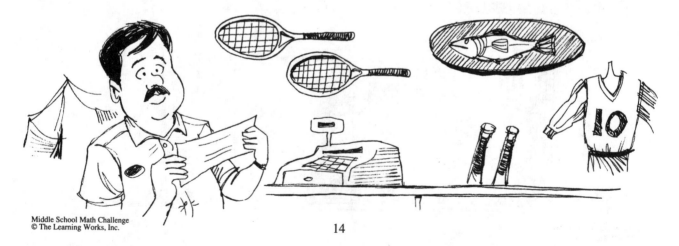

One Hundred Dollar Words

Each letter of the alphabet is worth a numerical point value as shown:

a	=	1	g	=	7	l	=	12	q	=	17	v	=	22
b	=	2	h	=	8	m	=	13	r	=	18	w	=	23
c	=	3	i	=	9	n	=	14	s	=	19	x	=	24
d	=	4	j	=	10	o	=	15	t	=	20	y	=	25
e	=	5	k	=	11	p	=	16	u	=	21	z	=	26
f	=	6											

Using this formula, the word *fuzzy* has a value of 104 points.

f = 6
u = 21
z = 26
z = 26
y = 25
_____
104 points

How many other words can you find that are worth 100 or more points?

Cross Up

Number of players: 2 to 3
Materials needed: colored marking pens for each player

Here is a road map of cities (circles) and nine freeways that connect them. Each player takes turns eliminating one of the nine freeways by coloring in the full length of the freeway he or she chooses. (Each player will need his or her own color.) The first player to color three freeways that enter the same city wins.

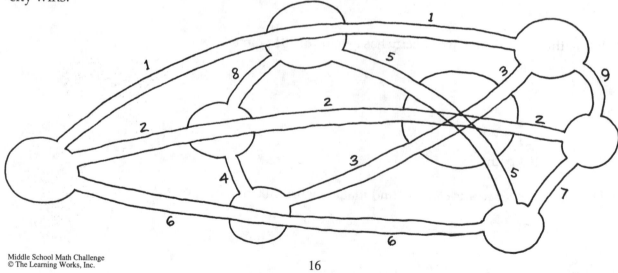

The Star

Place the integers from 1 through 12 in the circles of the star below. The sum of each of the six rows must total 26. To help you get started, four numbers have been placed on the star.

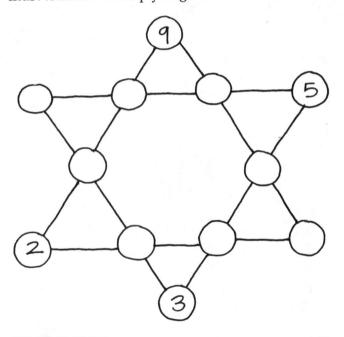

A Number Puzzle

Arrange the nine digits 1, 2, 3, 4, 5, 6, 7, 8, and 9 into three groups. Make one group of two digits, one group of three digits, and one group of four digits, so that when you multiply the first group of two times the second group of three you will get the third group of four.

Example: 39 x 186 = 7,254

There are six other possible combinations. Can you find all of them?

Not a Magic Square

In the example below, the digits 1 through 9 have been arranged so that the number that appears in the second row is twice that of the number in the first row. The number in the third row is three times the number in the first row. There are three other such arrangements. Find them and fill in the squares below.

Example:

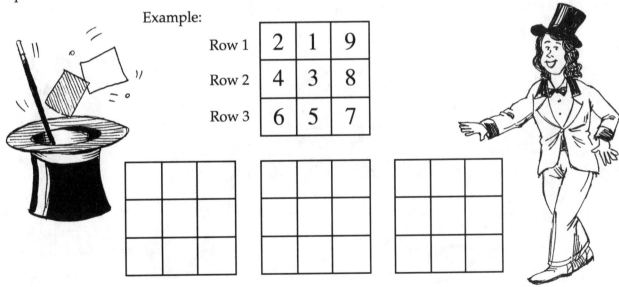

Row 1	2	1	9
Row 2	4	3	8
Row 3	6	5	7

An Odometer Oddity

A car's odometer measures how many miles the car has been driven. The other day while on a long trip, the odometer on our family car showed 87978, a number that reads the same backwards and forwards. I wondered how much time would pass until it occurred again. The first time it happened again was in two hours. A number appeared on the odometer that was the same read backwards and forwards. How fast was the car driven during those two hours?

Dividing a Square
into Four Equal Pieces

The two squares below have been divided into four congruent or equal pieces by following the solid lines. Can you find four other ways to solve this puzzle?

Examples:

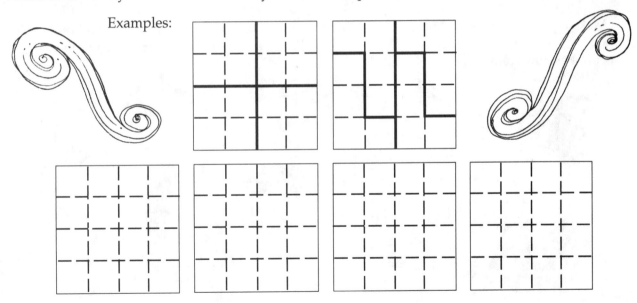

Make it Twenty

If you add four odd numbers, you can make 10 in three unique ways.

$$1 + 3 + 3 + 3 = 10$$
$$1 + 1 + 5 + 3 = 10$$
$$1 + 1 + 1 + 7 = 10$$

Make equations using addition and eight odd numbers to get 20. There are 11 solutions in all. (Note: $1 + 3 + 3 + 3 = 10$ is the same as $3 + 1 + 3 + 3 = 10$. Rearranging the order of the numbers does not count as new solutions.)

The Coin Dealer

A coin dealer had six old, silver dollars. Because of their age, they were each worth more than a dollar. When she put them on display in her coin case, she put the following price tags on them:

$15 $20 $16 $18 $31 $19

Two customers came into the coin shop wanting to buy one or more of the six coins. The first customer ended up paying exactly twice as much as the second customer for the coins he bought. One coin was left. Which coin did the coin dealer keep?

The Student Council Meeting

As president of the student body, I am on the student council and attend all meetings. At last night's meeting, there was an argument about the type of music we should have at the next dance: rap, top 40, or hard rock. Many of the student council members left. I was so angry that I had half a mind to leave myself. If I had gone, then two-thirds of the student council would have left. However, if I could have talked only two of the members into staying, one half of the student council would have been left and we would have had enough people to take a vote.

How many students were originally present?

Grandmother's Pearls

Grandmother has a beautiful strand of 33 pearls worth $65,000. On both sides of the strand, the pearls get larger as they go down the string from the clasp. The middle pearl is the most valuable. The pearls are arranged so that on one side each successive pearl is worth $100 more than the one before it, up to and including the middle pearl. On the other side, each successive pearl is worth $150 more than the one before it, up to and again including the middle pearl.

What is the value of the middle pearl?

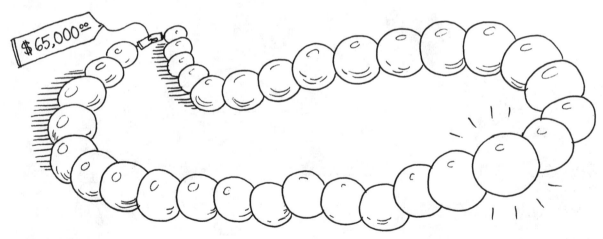

A Subtraction Game

Number of players: 2

The first player selects a number from 1 to 7 and subtracts it from 100. Player 2 also selects a number from 1 to 7, but subtracts it from the first player's remainder. The player who subtracts enough to leave 0 wins. An alternate way to play this game is to have the player who first reaches 0 declared the loser. Play this game a few times and see if you and a partner can come up with a winning strategy for both versions of the game.

Another Number Puzzle

Arrange the nine digits 1, 2, 3, 4, 5, 6, 7, 8, and 9 into three groups. The first group should contain one digit and the remaining two groups should each have four digits. Arrange the numbers so that when you multiply the group of one by the smaller of the two groups of four, you will get the larger group of four.

Example: $4 \times 1{,}963 = 7{,}852$

There is only one other arrangement that will yield such an equation. What is it?

Rumors at Rumor Junior High

At Rumor Junior High, news spreads quickly. When a student hears a rumor, he or she repeats it to two other students in 10 minutes and then tells no one else. A student heard a rumor at 8:30 A.M. How many students will know the rumor at 9:50 A.M.?

If 4,095 students know the rumor, what time is it? Describe the pattern.

Count the Overlapping Triangles

Add two lines to the drawing to make a total of 10 triangles, counting all the overlapping triangles.

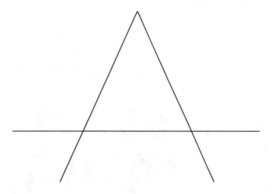

The Wicked King and His Plant

There was once a very wicked king. All he loved in life was his plant. He kept the plant close to his throne. He talked to it all day long. The king insisted that the plant get only four cups of water a day—no more and no less. If a servant didn't feed the plant properly, the king would punish the servant. Feeding the plant was a very unpopular job.

One day a young servant was asked to water the plant. He got so nervous that when he reached for the four-cup container, he dropped it and it broke. The same thing happened with the two- and one-cup containers. All he had left to work with were the three- and five-cup, unmarked containers. Nevertheless, he went to the river and came back with exactly four cups of water in the five-cup container. How did he do it?

The Letter M

Add three straight lines to the letter M to get nine triangles. The triangles cannot overlap.

Water Wonders

You are given a 10-cup container filled with water and two empty containers—one seven-cup and one three-cup. How can you move the water around so that there will be exactly five cups left in the 10-cup container when you are done?

The Circle Puzzle

This circle was divided into 16 pieces by making six cuts.

How can you make six cuts that yield more than 16 pieces?

The Underground Inspector

An underground railway inspector must travel between the stations on the map below to inspect all the tracks. Help him choose the shortest path between the stations. If each track segment is one mile long, how far must he travel to do this? (He can travel over some segments more than once.)

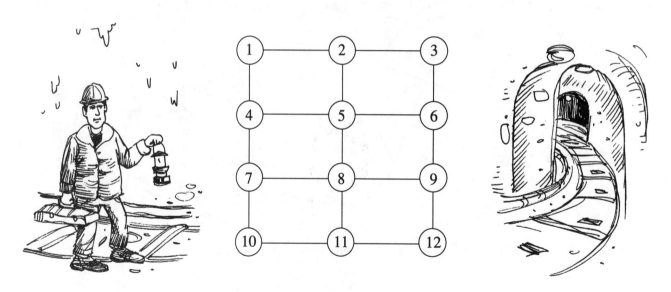

"Mom, I Need a Bike!"

"Mom, I wish you would buy me a bike," said six-year-old Elizabeth.

"I don't think you are old enough yet," her mother replied. "But I'll tell you what. When I am only three times as old as you are, I will get you one."

Today her mother's age is 26. When will the young girl get her bike?

Don't Buy Those Motorcycles!

A 13-year-old boy saved all his money and was finally able to buy two motorcycles. When his mother found out, she made him sell them both. He sold each for $600. He lost 20% on the expensive one and made a profit of 20% on the other one.

Did he make a profit or a loss on the whole transaction? How much did he make or lose?

How Old Was Mrs. Johnson?

When Mr. Johnson was married 18 years ago, he was three times as old as his wife. Today, he is only twice as old as his wife. How old was Mrs. Johnson when they got married?

Patterns With Meaning

Decipher each of the letter and number phrases below:

Example: **16 O in a P** stands for **16 ounces in a pint**.

1. 26 L in the A
2. 12 M in a Y
3. 4 Q in a G
4. 36 B K on a P
5. F T 13th
6. The 12 D of C
7. 7 W of the W
8. K H the 8th
9. The 10 C
10. S W and the 7 D
11. 9 P on a B T
12. The 3 W M
13. 366 D in a L Y

14. 2,000 P in 1 T
15. 40 D and N of the G F
16. 13 S on the A F
17. 13 in a B D
18. 1,001 A N
19. 100 Y in a C
20. 60 S in a M
21. The 100 Y W
22. 101 D
23. 3 P in a H G
24. 18 H on a G C
25. 50 S in the U.S.
26. 24 H in a D

Gender Guess

I have two children. They aren't both boys.
What is the probability that both children are girls?

My best friend has two children. The older is a boy.
What is the probability that both children are boys?

What's the Number?

I am thinking of a three-digit number. If you subtract 5 from it, the result is divisible by 5. If you subtract 6 from it, the result is divisible by 6. If you subtract 7 from it, the result is divisible by 7. What is the smallest number that will satisfy these conditions?

Diffy

Instructions:

1. Photocopy the grid on page 133 onto a separate sheet of paper. Fill in the outermost corner circles with any four positive integers. In the example, the numbers 10, 7, 5, and 6 were chosen.
2. Fill in the inner circles by subtracting the smaller from the larger number in the circles that are on the straight line and on either side of the inner circle.

   Example:

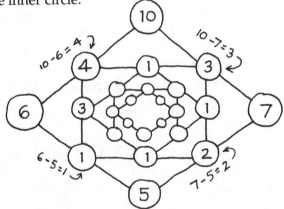

3. Continue inward until you get all zeros.

The object of the game is to complete as many levels as possible. Carefully choose your outermost numbers, the first four, to allow you to avoid zeros and keep playing as long as you can.

Nim

Number of players: 2

One possible playing board is shown below. The number of rows you use and the number of lines in each row can change from game to game.

row 1 | | | | | | |
row 2 | | | | | | |

Rules:
1. During a move a player can place an "X" on 1, 2, or 3 line segments in any one row.
2. Each player must place at least one "X" during his or her turn.
3. The player who places an "X" on the last line segment loses.

Try to come up with a plan that will allow you to avoid placing that last "X" and losing.

Optional playing board designs:

| | | |
| | | | |

    | | |
| | | | |
| | | | |

    | | |
| | |
| | | | |

    | | |
| | | | |
| | | | | |

Absolutely Perfect Numbers

A number is perfect if it equals the sum of its factors,
excluding the number itself but including the number 1.

Examples:

6 is perfect because 1 + 2 + 3 = 6.
28 is perfect because 1 + 2 + 4 + 7 + 14 = 28.

Show that 496 is a perfect number.
Find other perfect numbers.

Number Buddies

The numbers 220 and 284 are buddies. They are buddies because:

1. The factors of 220 (less than 220) are:
   1, 2, 4, 5, 10, 11, 20, 22, 44, 55, and 110
   and
   $1 + 2 + 4 + 5 + 10 + 11 + 20 + 22 + 44 + 55 + 110 = 284$.

2. Furthermore, the factors of 284 are:
   1, 2, 4, 71, and 142
   and
   $1 + 2 + 4 + 71 + 142 = 220$.

Show how 1,184 and 1,210 are buddies.
Can you find the buddy of 496?
How many other buddy pairs can you find?

Triangle Numbers

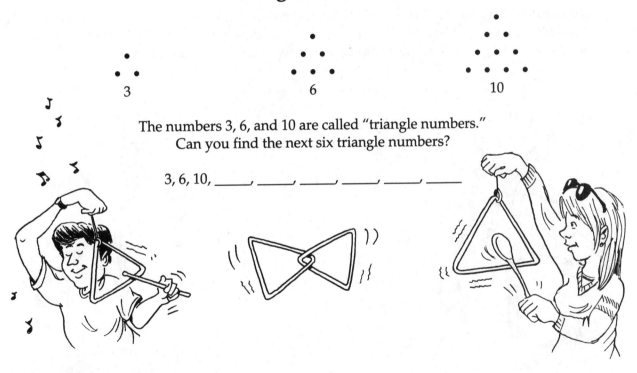

3

6

10

The numbers 3, 6, and 10 are called "triangle numbers."
Can you find the next six triangle numbers?

3, 6, 10, _____, _____, _____, _____, _____, _____

Wet Paint!

Each of the rectangular floor tiles below has been painted in the center. Start at the bottom left corner (1) and go to the upper right corner (2) by walking along the edges of the rectangles. Find the longest path without going along any edge twice. How long is the longest path?

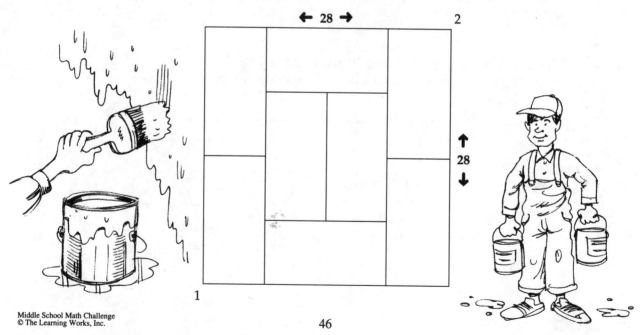

First Nine Counting Numbers

Fill in the squares below with the digits 1, 2, 3, 4, 5, 6, 7, 8, and 9. Use each number only once.

Make up a similar problem to challenge your friends.

Triangle Numbers II

The numbers in the sequence below are called "triangle numbers."

1, 3, 6, 10, 15, 21, 28, 36, 45, 55, 66, 78, ...

Each of these can be made into a triangle.

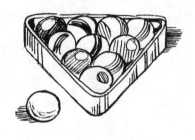

These numbers have many interesting properties. For example, what happens if successive triangle numbers are added together? Complete the pattern below.

$$1 \quad 3 \quad 6 \quad 10 \quad 15 \quad 21 \quad 28 \quad 36 \quad 45 \quad 55$$

$$\diagdown + \diagup \ \diagdown + \diagup \ \diagdown + \diagup \ \diagdown + \diagup \ \diagdown + \diagup \ \diagdown + \diagup \ \diagdown + \diagup \ \diagdown + \diagup \ \diagdown + \diagup$$

$$4 \quad 9 \quad 16 \quad 25 \quad 36 \quad 49 \quad \underline{\quad} \quad \underline{\quad} \quad \underline{\quad}$$

Notice also:

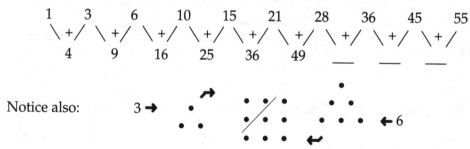

Find another property that triangle numbers share.

Squares on a Table

Eight identical square pieces of paper are placed on a desk. They overlap each other as shown. Sheet 1 is on top and is completely visible. All the other pieces are only partly exposed. Number the squares in order from the second layer from the top (#2) to the bottom layer (#8).

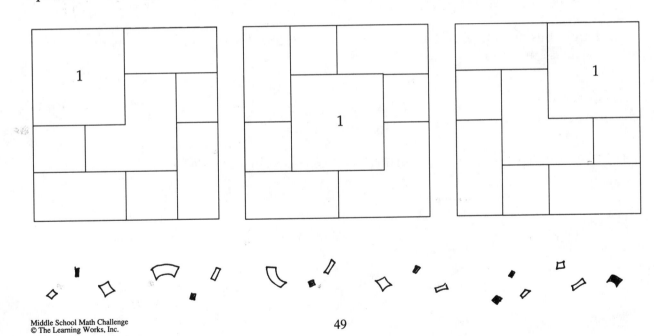

Geometry

How Many Ways?

The three points below make up an **isosceles triangle**. They can be connected in only one way with straight lines without lifting the pencil.

The four points that make up a square can be connected with straight lines in only two unique ways. (The lines can cross).

Note: is the same as 2, just turned on its side.

The five points that make up a pentagon can be connected in only four unique ways.

In how many unique ways can a hexagon be connected? Remember, your pen or pencil must not leave the paper and you may only visit each point once.

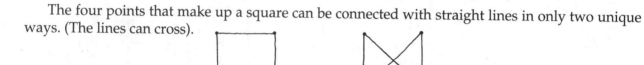

Pretty Numbers

Pretty numbers are numbers that are **palindromes**. Palindromes read the same backwards and forwards. Just as the words "dad," "radar," and "civic" are palindromes, the numbers 121 and 7337 are palindromes, also known as "pretty numbers." Any number can be made pretty by reversing its digits and adding the reversed digit number to the original number enough times.

Consider 13, 16, and 29.

13	16	29
+ 31	+ 61	+ 92
44	77	121

The numbers 13, 16, and 29 are pretty at level 1, or P1.

Consider 57 and 19.

57	132	19	110
+ 75	+ 231	+ 91	+ 011
132	363	110	121

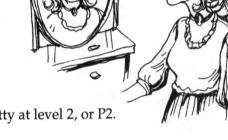

Since it took two "reverse and adds," 57 and 19 are pretty at level 2, or P2.

Find a number between 10 and 100 that is pretty after five or more "reverse and adds."

Plus or Minus

If you place seven signs, plus (+) or minus (–), between the digits 1, 2, 3, 4, 5, 6, 7, 8, and 9, you can make an equation that equals 100.

$$1 + 2 + 3 - 4 + 5 + 6 + 78 + 9 = 100$$

Can you do it with only three plus or minus signs?

Every Wall Has a Door

Below is the floor plan to a strange house. Each wall in every room has a door. Trace a path through each room so that each door is passed through only once. You can start or end inside or outside any room.

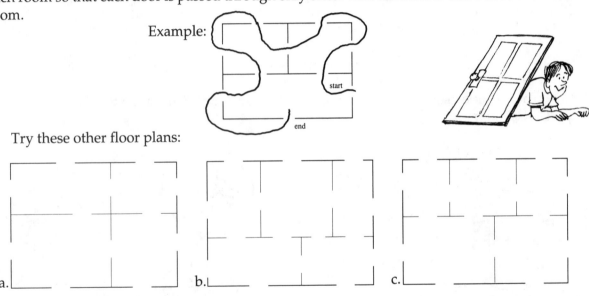

Try these other floor plans:

a.   b.   c.

Design a room and try it on a friend.

Pluses

You can place addition signs between the digits of 9, 8, 7, 6, 5, 4, 3, 2, and 1 to make a total of 99. One solution is $9 + 8 + 7 + 6 + 5 + 43 + 21 = 99$.

Can you find another?

Now place addition signs between the digits 1, 2, 3, 4, 5, 6, and 7 to make a total of 100. There are two possible solutions.

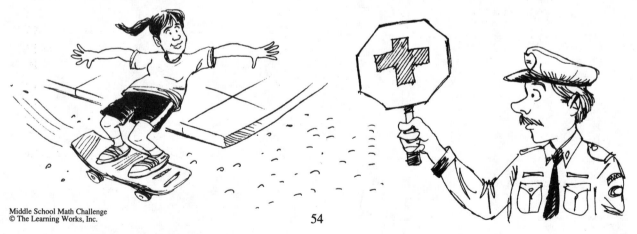

Four Fours

Use four fours with math operations, symbols, and parentheses (if necessary) to form **all** the integers from 0 to 50. Do your work on a separate piece of paper. Fill in your answers on this page. Two have been done for you.

Hints: $4! = 1 \times 2 \times 3 \times 4 = 24$
$\sqrt{4} = 2$
$4 \div .4 = 10$

$4 - 4 + 4 - 4 = 0$	$= 11$	$= 21$	$= 31$	$= 41$
$= 1$	$= 12$	$= 22$	$= 32$	$= 42$
$= 2$	$= 13$	$= 23$	$= 33$	$= 43$
$= 3$	$= 14$	$= 24$	$= 34$	$= 44$
$= 4$	$= 15$	$= 25$	$= 35$	$= 45$
$= 5$	$= 16$	$= 26$	$= 36$	$= 46$
$= 6$	$= 17$	$= 27$	$= 37$	$= 47$
$= 7$	$= 18$	$= 28$	$= 38$	$= 48$
$= 8$	$= 19$	$= 29$	$= 39$	$= 49$
$= 9$	$= 20$	$= 30$	$= 40$	$(4! \bullet \sqrt{4}) + 4 - \sqrt{4} = 50$
$= 10$				

It Makes One Hundred

Using exactly five 5's, construct an expression that will equal 100. You may use the operation symbols +, −, x, and ÷ as well as parentheses or brackets.

Example: $(5 + 5 + 5 + 5) \times 5 = 100$

There are two other such expressions. Can you find them?

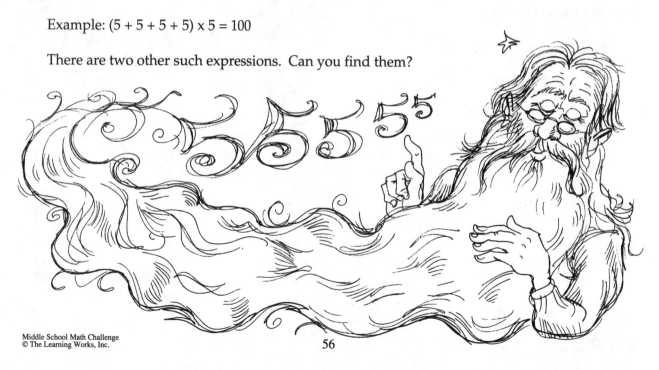

A Magic Triangle

1, 2, and 3 are placed on the vertices of a triangle as shown below. Arrange the numbers 4, 5, 6, 7, 8, and 9 along the sides of the triangle (using each only once) so that the sum of each side equals 17. There are two solutions.

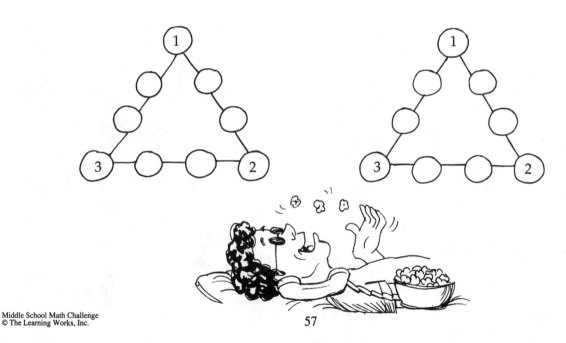

The First 19 Numbers

Place the numbers 1 through 19 in the circles so that the numbers in the three circles on every straight line total 30.

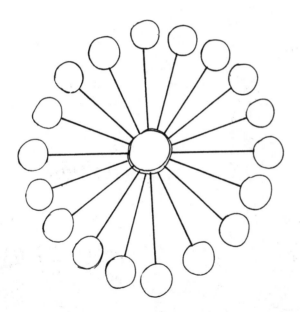

The Clock Face

Divide the clock face with two straight lines so that
the sum of the numbers in each of three parts are equal.

Bridges

Number of players: 2

Player 1 connects any two ▲'s with a line, either vertical or horizontal. Player 1's objective is to make a continuous line connecting the left and right side of the grid. Player 2 in his or her turn connects any two ●'s, with a line, either vertical or horizontal. Player 2's objective is to make a continuous line connecting the top and bottom of the grid. The players take turns drawing one line each time and no line is permitted to cross any other line. The first player to reach his or her objective wins. A playing board that you can photocopy appears on page 134.

In this example, player 2 wins:

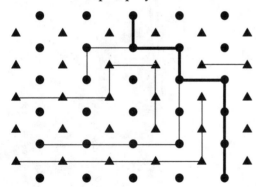

The Even Number Wins

Number of players: 2
Materials needed: 27 paper clips

During each player's turn, he or she picks up 1, 2, 3, or 4 paper clips from the pile of 27. The player who finishes the game with an even number of paper clips wins. Can you devise a way to win if you go first? Play this game a few times and try to devise a strategy to win.

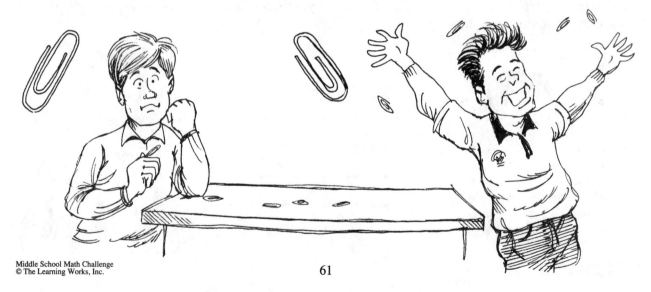

Boxes

Number of players: 2

During his or her turn, each player makes a straight line connecting any two adjacent dots, either horizontally or vertically. If a player completes a box (all four sides), he places his or her initials inside it and then adds another straight line. The first player continues his or her turn until no new boxes can be made. Then, it is the second player's turn. The player that completes the most boxes wins.

Here is a partially completed game. (Note that your game board may be of any size.) A playing board that you can reproduce appears on page 135.

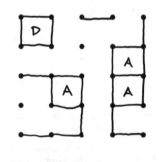

How Old?

When my dad was 31, I was 8. Today he is twice as old as I am.
How old am I, and how old is my dad?

Five Gold Chains

You are given five large, gold chains each consisting of three links. It costs 50 cents to break a link and one dollar to join it again. Your job is to find the least expensive method of joining all five chain segments into a single chain.

Mail on the Luxury Liner

A luxury liner left for a long voyage. When the ship was 360 miles from shore, a mail delivery helicopter, which could travel 10 times the speed of the liner, took off after it. How far from the shore will the helicopter be when it catches up with the liner?

The Seven Bulldogs

The pen below contains seven bulldogs. Draw three straight lines for fences so that each dog is enclosed in a separate yard. (The dogs will not move while you are building your fences.)

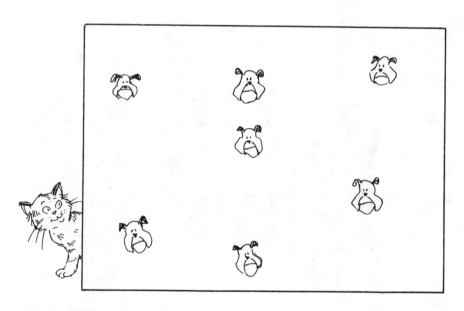

Eleven Separate Enclosures

A farmer has a square field containing 11 large oak trees. She wants to divide the field into 11 enclosures so that each has one shade tree for her cattle. Divide the field using four straight lines to indicate where the fences will be built.

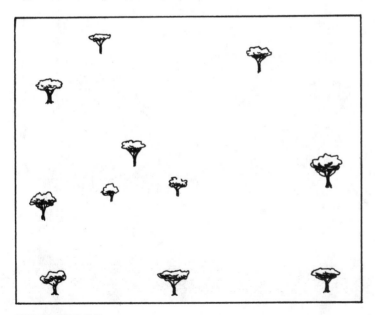

A Topsy Turvy Year

Find the most recent year that reads the same upside down as it does right side up. For example, 1881 is the same upside down as it is right side up.

Division

Find the largest number that can be divided into 701, 1,059, 1,417, and 2,312 and leaves the same remainder. Trial and error will work, but there is a much simpler way to find the number if one just thinks a while first.

Proof That 1 + 1 = 3

Let x = 1 and y = 2, then:

x + y = 3

Multiply each side by 2x − 3:

$(2x - 3) \bullet (x + y) = (2x - 3) \bullet (3)$

$2x^2 - 3x + 2xy - 3y = 6x - 9$

Add 3y − 3x to both sides:

$2x^2 - 3x + 2xy - 3y + (3y - 3x) = 6x - 9 + (3y - 3x)$

$2x^2 - 6x + 2xy = 3x + 3y - 9$

Factor both sides:

$2x(x - 3 + y) = 3(x + y - 3)$

OR

$2x(x + y - 3) = 3(x + y - 3)$

Divide both sides by (x + y − 3):

2x = 3

But then:

x + x = 3

with x = 1

Therefore: 1 + 1 = 3

Where did our proof go wrong?

Stack It Again, Sam!

Consider an ordinary sheet of paper (white, lined, three-holed, .005 inches thick). Suppose you tore it in half and stacked the pieces to double the thickness. Imagine that you were to tear this new stack in half and pile the pieces so as to double the thickness again. How tall do you think the stack would be if you tore and doubled it 50 times? Give your estimate in *miles!*

Cubes from Squares

There are many ways to place six squares side by side so that when they are folded they will make a cube. For example:

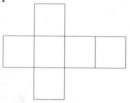

Use the grid at the right to trace as many patterns as you can that, when folded, will form a cube. When you finish, cut out your patterns and see if they work. Note however that

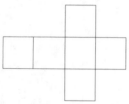

is the same as the example above, only rotated, and therefore does not count as a second solution.

Weird Number Patterns

Try to complete the following pattern. Then use your calculator to verify your results.

$11 \times 11 = 121$

$111 \times 111 = 12{,}321$

$1{,}111 \times 1{,}111 = 1{,}234{,}321$

$11{,}111 \times 11{,}111 = \underline{\hspace{2cm}}$

$111{,}111 \times 111{,}111 = \underline{\hspace{2cm}}$

$1{,}111{,}111 \times 1{,}111{,}111 = \underline{\hspace{2cm}}$

$11{,}111{,}111 \times 11{,}111{,}111 = \underline{\hspace{2cm}}$

$111{,}111{,}111 \times \underline{\hspace{2cm}} = \underline{\hspace{2cm}}$

Now try:

$9 \times 9 + 7 = 88$

$98 \times 9 + 6 = 888$

$987 \times 9 + 5 = 8{,}888$

$9{,}876 \times 9 + 4 = 88{,}888$

$98{,}765 \times 9 + 3 = \underline{\hspace{2cm}}$

$\underline{\hspace{2cm}} \times 9 + 2 = \underline{\hspace{2cm}}$

$\underline{\hspace{2cm}} \times 9 + 1 = \underline{\hspace{2cm}}$

$\underline{\hspace{2cm}} \times 9 + 0 = \underline{\hspace{2cm}}$

Howlers

Consider the following fraction reductions:

$$\frac{16}{64} = \frac{1}{4} \qquad \frac{19}{95} = \frac{1}{5} \qquad \frac{26}{65} = \frac{2}{5} \qquad \frac{49}{98} = \frac{4}{8} = \frac{1}{2}$$

Note also that these results can be obtained using a special method of cancellation:

$$\frac{1\cancel{6}}{\cancel{6}4} = \frac{1}{4} \qquad \frac{19}{9\cancel{5}} = \frac{1}{5} \qquad \frac{2\cancel{6}}{\cancel{6}5} = \frac{2}{5} \qquad \frac{4\cancel{9}}{\cancel{9}8} = \frac{4}{8} = \frac{1}{2}$$

This will *not* work with all fractions—only with very special ones called "howlers." Can you find another fraction that has this property? (Hint: try three-digit numbers in the numerator and denominator.) Multiples of 11 do not count; they are considered trivial, for example, $\frac{55}{55} = \frac{5}{5} = 1$.

Letters for Digits

In this problem each letter stands for one digit and has the same value throughout the equation. Find the appropriate digits to make the following subtraction problem work.

$$
\begin{array}{r}
S\ T\ O\ P \\
-\ T\ O\ P\ S \\
\hline
P\ O\ T\ S
\end{array}
$$

The Diamond Ring

Kelly can buy a pearl necklace and a diamond ring for $700. She can buy a gold pen and a pearl necklace for $600. She can buy a diamond ring and a gold pen for $500. How much would Kelly have to pay for the diamond ring alone?

Two Pages in a Book

Susan closed her eyes and opened her algebra book. After checking the page numbers, she noticed that their product was 650. To which two page numbers did Susan open her book?

Playing With Sugar Cubes

The number of sugar cubes equal to a perfect square can be used to form a square.

Example: $2^2 = 4$ and $3^2 = 9$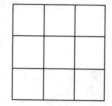

The number of sugar cubes equal to a perfect cube can be used to form a cube.

Example: $2^3 = 8$ and $3^3 =$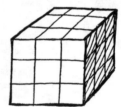

Can you find the smallest number of sugar *cubes* (that is, more than one) that can be used to form either a square or a cube?

More Addition

Fill in the boxes with whole numbers less than 10 so that the addition will be correct. Now multiply the numbers you placed in the boxes.

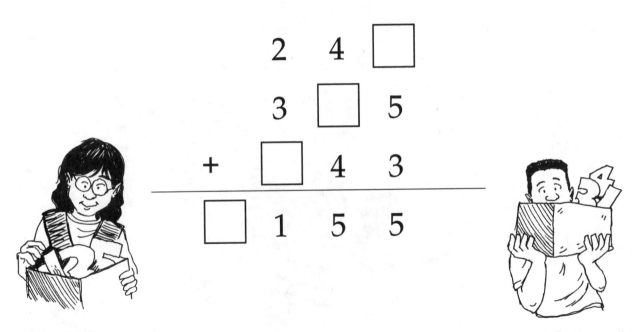

Prime Years

A prime number is a natural number divisible by no integer other than 1 and itself. There is an infinite quantity of prime numbers. The largest known prime number, as of February 1992, is

$$2^{756,839} - 1 \quad \text{(It has 227,832 digits!)}$$

During the final 50 years of this millennium there are seven years that are prime numbers. One of them is 1999. What are the other six?

Paper Strips

Take four strips of paper, all 10 inches in length but having differing widths of one inch, two inches, three inches, and four inches. Lay them out on a desk as shown below. How much area of the desk will be covered?

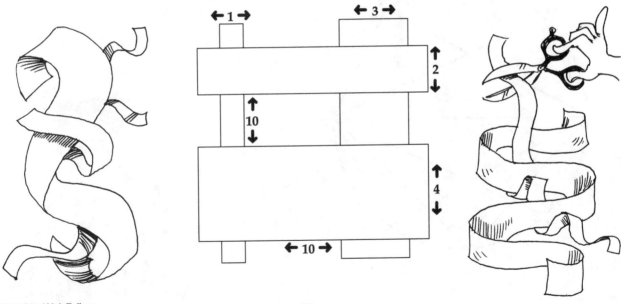

Inscribed Angles

Below is a circle with five inscribed angles. Each is contained in one half of the circle. What is the measure of each angle?

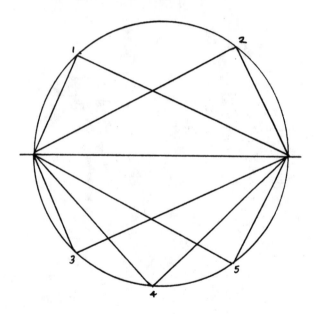

Number Sequences

Continue the following sequences:

4, 25, 64, 121, 196, 289, _____

11, 2S, 3E, 4P, 5Z, 6Ð, _____

2, 5, 10, 17, 26, 37, _____

2, 4, 8, 16, 32, 64, _____

1, 3, 7, 15, 31, 63, _____

0, 1, 1, 2, 3, 5, _____

–9, –2, 17, 54, 115, 206, _____

3, 6, 10, 15, 21, 28, _____

The First Six Non-Zero Digits

Complete the multiplication problem below by filling in the boxes with the numbers 1 through 6. Use each number only once.

A Fibonacci Surprise

A Fibonacci sequence is made up of terms created by adding the two previous terms in the sequence starting with one.

1, 1, 2, 3, 5, 8, 13, 21, 34, 55, 89, 144, 233, 377, 610, 987, 1,597, 2,584, 4,181, 6,765, 10,946...

Can you show that no matter where you start, when you sum the next 10 numbers in a Fibonacci sequence, your answer will always be 11 times the seventh term from where you started?

Aristotle's Wheel

This puzzle dates back to Aristotle, the famous Greek mathematician.

A wheel can be thought of as two circles with the same center.

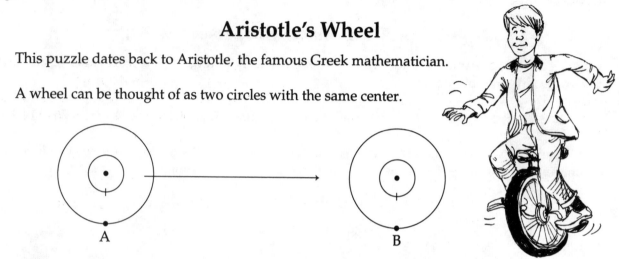

The wheel above moves from A to B. It rotates once. The distance from A to B is the circumference of the larger circle. Since the smaller circle also rotates once and also travels the distance from A to B, its circumference must also be equal to the distance from A to B. But the smaller circle clearly has a smaller circumference than the larger one. What is wrong here?

A Flexagon

This type of topological puzzle is made from paper and has a varying number of faces. The numbers on the faces are brought into view by flexing the paper construction vertically.

Using the information below, you can make a "tri-tetra" flexagon. The "tri" stands for the number of faces, in this case three. The "tetra" stands for the number of sides, in this case 12. This construction is best made on one-inch grid construction paper.

Front:

Back:

You should end up with 2's on the front and 1's on the back. To have the numbers change, simply fold the square vertically in the middle.

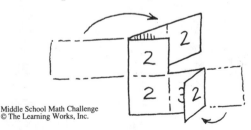
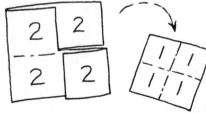

Twin Primes

Twin primes are prime numbers that are only separated by one number. For example, 3 and 5 are twin primes; 5 and 7 are also twin primes. The largest known twin primes, $1{,}706{,}595 \times 2^{11{,}235} - 1$ and $1{,}706{,}595 \times 2^{11{,}235} + 1$, were discovered in August of 1989 by a team of computer scientists in California.

There are eight prime pairs between 3 and 100. You already know two of them: 3 and 5, and 5 and 7. What are the other six?

Finding Pi With Probability

Pi is the ratio of a circle's circumference to its diameter (i.e., Pi = circumference/diameter). There are many methods to approximate the value of Pi. The most accurate value of Pi was discovered on November 19, 1989 using a high-speed computer. Pi was calculated to over 1,073,740,000 places!

One of the most surprising methods to calculate Pi was discovered by the French naturalist Count Buffon in the 18th century. Using a needle and a blank sheet of paper, follow the steps below to see how Buffon calculated Pi using probability.

Steps:
1. Measure the length of the needle. Draw lines across the paper so that the lines are separated by the length of the needle. Draw as many lines as you can.
2. Drop the needle onto the paper from a height of approximately one foot.
3. Make 1,000 drops and count the number of times the needle crosses one of the lines. Let that number be "N."
4. If you divide 2,000 by that number "N" you will get an approximation of Pi. In other words, Pi is about 2,000/N.

The Sieve of Eratosthenes

Prime numbers play an important role in the field of mathematics. They also figure prominently in cryptography, the science of making and breaking secret messages. Eratosthenes, a Greek mathematician, discovered a method to "sieve," or filter out, prime numbers from other numbers. This method was used to find all prime numbers less than 30 in the grid below. The prime numbers are circled.

Using this method, continue working and determine the number of prime numbers less than 100.

X̶	(2)	(3)	X̶	(5)	X̶	(7)	X̶	X̶	1̶0̶	(11)	1̶2̶	(13)	1̶4̶	1̶5̶	1̶6̶	(17)	1̶8̶	(19)	2̶0̶
2̶1̶	2̶2̶	(23)	2̶4̶	2̶5̶	2̶6̶	2̶7̶	2̶8̶	(29)	3̶0̶	31	32	33	34	35	36	37	38	39	40
41	42	43	44	45	46	47	48	49	50	51	52	53	54	55	56	57	58	59	60
61	62	63	64	65	66	67	68	69	70	71	72	73	74	75	76	77	78	79	80
81	82	83	84	85	86	87	88	89	90	91	92	93	94	95	96	97	98	99	100

Steps:
1. Start with 2 (1 is not prime by agreement).
2. Circle 2, then cross out all multiples of 2.
3. Circle 3, then cross out all multiples of 3.
4. Go to the next number that is not crossed out, circle it, then cross out all multiples of that number.
5. Continue with this process until all of the numbers are crossed out or circled.

Connect the Shapes

Given the rectangle below, your job is to connect each shape with its pair, drawing a line. (Note: The lines need not be straight, but they cannot cross each other or travel outside the rectangle. They also may not go around the back, that is, between the wall and the object.)

A Five-Digit Number

Below is a five-digit number.

12R3T

Find the digits to replace R and T so that the number will be divisible by both 9 and 4. R, however, cannot equal T!

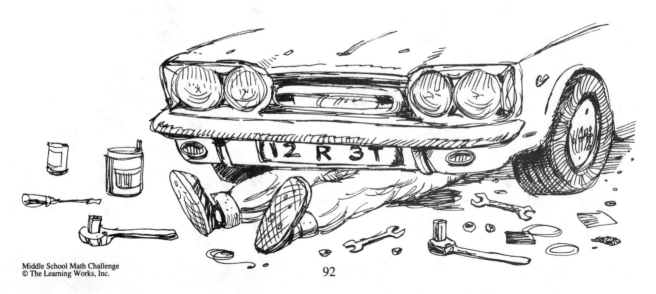

Making Change

You reach into your pocket and find two pennies, two nickels, and one dime. How many different amounts of money can you make using the five coins? (Note that two nickels is the same as one dime.)

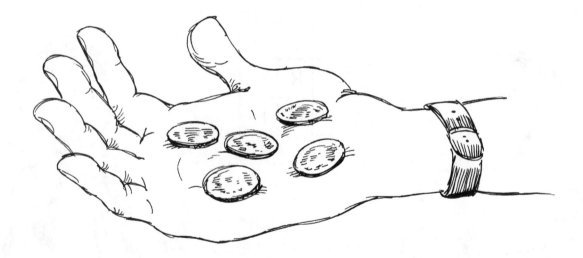

The Magic Square

In "magic squares" each row, each diagonal, and each column must add up to the same number. Find R in the magic square below.

11	T	V
S	R	W
14	Q	19

Find the Perimeter

Find the perimeter of the figure below. All of the angles shown are 90°.

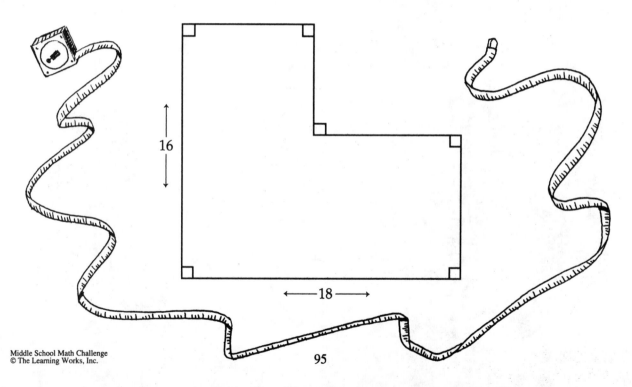

It's the Product

R2
x 7R
―――――
6,396

Find R so that the product will be correct.

Bikes and Trikes

The local bike shop ordered 19 wheels. The shop owner wanted to make seven bicycles and/or tricycles from them. How many of each type must he make to use up all of the wheels?

One Billion Dollars

The value of gold and the value of silver change almost daily. The price is usually found with the stock price information in your local newspaper. If one dollar bill weighs 1/40th of an ounce (40 dollar bills weigh about one ounce), which of the following will weigh more?

(a) one billion dollars worth of gold
(b) one billion dollars in dollar bills
(c) one billion dollars worth of silver

A Quarter

How many different ways can you make change for a quarter?

Candy Bars

One child said to another, "If you give me just one of your candy bars, then we will both have the same number of candy bars." The other child replied, "No, you give me one of your candy bars and then I'll have twice as many as you have." How many candy bars does each child have?

Jogging Shoes

Maria jogs a lot. In fact, she has 10 pairs of jogging shoes in her closet. Yesterday evening she went to her closet to get a pair of jogging shoes for a night run. The light in her closet wouldn't work. What is the smallest number of shoes Maria will need to get out to ensure that she has one matching pair?

Count Your Diagonals

A square has two diagonals.

A pentagon has five diagonals.

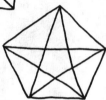

How many more diagonals can you find in an octagon (eight sides) than in a heptagon (seven sides)?

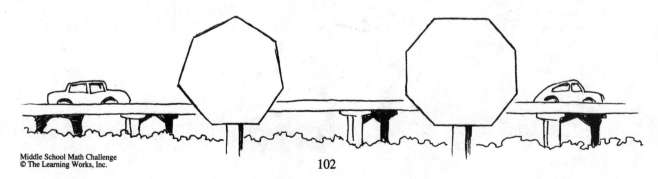

The Planet Zot

During my last visit to the Planet Zot, my friend Zak was counting his marbles. He started: "Ze, zi, zip, zum, zut, zut-ze, zut-zi, zut-zip, zut-zum, zut-zut, zut-zut-ze, . . ."

With this method of counting, what word would Zak use to count his twentieth marble?

A Fifty Cent Piece

How many different ways can you make change for a fifty cent piece?

Big Money

Diamond Jim has money coming out of his ears. When he arranged his dollar bills into stacks of six, he had three bills left over. When he made stacks of eight, he had seven bills left over. When he organized his money into stacks of five, he had four left over. Assuming Jim has less than 100 one dollar bills, how many would he have left over if made stacks of nine?

A Number Pyramid

Shown below is a number pyramid. The first five levels have been provided. Can you find the fifth item in the thirteenth level?

```
                    1
                 2  3  4
              5  6  7  8  9
          10  11  12  13  14  15  16
      17  18  19  20  21  22  23  24  25
  26  27 . . .
```

Don't Lift Your Pen!

Can you draw the following figure without lifting your pen from the page or tracing over the same line twice?

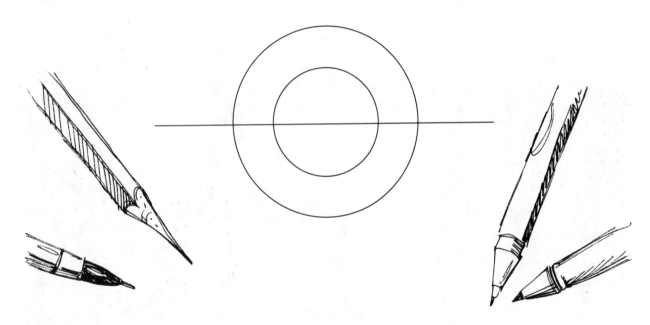

Home Building

Six carpenters can build six houses in six days. Twelve apprentices can build 12 houses in 12 days. How many houses can 12 carpenters and 12 apprentices build in 12 days?

How Many Triangles?

How many triangles can you count in the figure below?

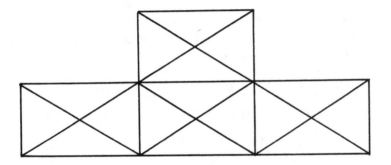

Tip Top

Number of players: 2 to 4

This game can be played with four to eight students. A digit is chosen from 2 through 9. This is the "key digit." Going in a clockwise direction and starting with the number 1, each student calls out a number one higher than the number previously called out, *or* the student calls out "tip," "top," or "tip top." The student calls out "tip" if the unit digit of her number is the same as the key digit (for example, 6 is the unit digit of 16). She calls out "top" if her number is divisible by the key digit. She calls out "tip top" if both conditions hold true. Below is an example with 4 as the key digit.

1	2	3	"TIP TOP"	5	6	7	"TOP"	9
10	11	"TOP"	13	"TIP"	15	"TOP"	17	18
19	"TOP"	21	22	23	"TIP TOP"	25	26	27
"TOP"	29 . . .							

When a student calls out the wrong response, she is eliminated for the remainder of that game. The game continues to successively higher numbers until only one player is left.

ANSWER KEY

Only Primes 2, 3, 5, or 7—page 7

Consider the last digits of the first three lines—a, b, and c. If a • b = c, c must be 5 and a or b must be 2 or 3.

$$\begin{array}{r} 775 \\ \times\ 33 \\ \hline 2325 \\ 2325 \\ \hline 25{,}575 \end{array}$$

A Crystal Lattice—page 8

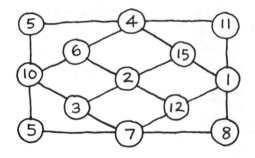

It's Raining! It's Pouring!—page 9

Absolutely not. In 96 hours, it will be 12:00 midnight and dark.

Now That's Some Gas Mileage—page 10

Invention 1: 1.00 − .35 = .65 remaining fuel cost
Invention 2: 1.00 − .40 = .60 remaining fuel cost
Invention 3: 1.00 − .25 = .75 remaining fuel cost
Since these are all independent events, to get the combined result we must multiply the results

.65 • .60 • .75 = .2925 total remaining fuel costs
Therefore, the savings is 1.00 − .2925 = 70.25% savings.

My Family—page 11

There are four brothers and three sisters.

ANSWER KEY

What Happened to the Extra Dollar?—page 13

This is an accounting problem. The problem says to add $2.00 but, in fact, the $2.00 should be subtracted from the $57.00. Once the manger returned the $5.00, the number you are trying to account for is $55.00, not $60.00.

A Bad Check—page 14

Pump cost   = $9.00
Money cost = $10.00
Total loss   = $19.00

One Hundred Dollar Words—page 15

Try the word "straws."

Cross Up—page 16

Once this simple game is played for a few rounds, it can be seen to be equivalent to tic-tac-toe.

The Star—page 17

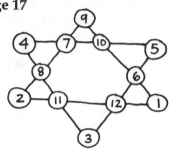

A Number Puzzle—page 18

$12 \times 483 = 5{,}796$ $18 \times 297 = 5{,}346$
$42 \times 138 = 5{,}796$ $28 \times 157 = 4{,}396$
$27 \times 198 = 5{,}346$ $48 \times 159 = 7{,}632$

Not a Magic Square—page 19

1	9	2
3	8	4
5	7	6

2	7	3
5	4	3
8	1	9

3	2	7
6	5	4
9	8	1

ANSWER KEY

An Odometer Oddity—page 20

The second and fourth digit must change to 8. The third digit must change to 0. We get:

$$88,088 \\ -87,978 \over 110$$ and $110 \div 2 = 55$

Dividing a Square into Four, Equal Pieces—page 21

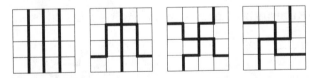

Make it Twenty—page 22

If you use the numbers 15, 17, or 19, you won't have room for the other seven numbers. Start at 13:

$$1 + 1 + 1 + 1 + 1 + 1 + 1 + 13 = 20$$
$$1 + 1 + 1 + 1 + 1 + 1 + 3 + 11 = 20$$
$$1 + 1 + 1 + 1 + 1 + 1 + 5 + 9 = 20$$

$$1 + 1 + 1 + 1 + 1 + 3 + 3 + 9 = 20$$
etc.
$$1 + 1 + 1 + 1 + 1 + 1 + 7 + 7 = 20$$
$$1 + 1 + 1 + 1 + 1 + 3 + 5 + 7 = 20$$

The Coin Dealer—page 23

$18 + 15 = 33$ and $16 + 19 + 31 = 66$

The store owner kept the $20.00 piece.

The Student Council Meeting—page 24

Eighteen students were originally present. During the exodus, 11 left. If 12 had gone, two-thirds would have left. If nine had gone, however, we would have lost only half of the original number.

Let x be the number of students who left.

Let y be the number of students originally present.

$$x - 2 = \frac{1}{2}y \qquad \frac{2}{3}y - 1 - 2 = \frac{1}{2}y$$
$$x + 1 = \frac{2}{3}y \qquad \frac{2}{3}y - \frac{1}{2}y = 3$$
$$x = \frac{2}{3}y - 1 \qquad \frac{4}{6}y - \frac{3}{6}y = 3$$
$$\frac{1}{6}y = 3$$
$$y = 18$$

ANSWER KEY

Grandmother's Pearls—page 25

Let x be the first pearl on the side that increases in value by 100. Let y be the first pearl on the side that increases in value by 150. The big pearl is $x + 1,600$

or $y + 2,400$, so $x + 1,600 = y + 2,400$

$$x = y + 800$$

By adding both sides and the middle pearl we get

$x + (x + 100) + (x + 200) + (x + 300) + (x + 400)$
$+ (x + 500) + (x + 600) + (x + 700) + (x + 800) +$
$(x + 900) + (x + 1,000) + (x + 1,100) + (x + 1,200)$
$+ (x + 1,300) + (x + 1,400) + (x + 1,500) + y +$
$(y + 150) + (y + 300) + (y + 450) + (y + 600) +$
$(y + 750) + (y + 900) + (y + 1,050) + (y + 1,200) +$
$(y + 1,350) + (y + 1,500) + (y + 1,650) +$
$(y + 1,800) + (y + 1,950) + (y + 2,100) +$
$(y + 2,250) + x + 1,600 = 17x + 16y + 31,600$.

But this is 65,000, so

$17x + 16y + 31,600 = 65,000$ and $x = y + 800$, so

$17 (y + 800) + 16y = 33,400$

$$33y = 19,800$$

$y = 600$, so $x = 1,400$

and the middle pearl is worth $3,000.

A Subtraction Game—page 26

The winning strategy for "zero wins" involves choosing a number that will sum with your opponent's number to make 8. This will force a win once you reach a multiple of 8. If "zero loses" is your game, then you want multiples of 8 plus 1.

Another Number Puzzle—page 27

$4 \times 1,738 = 6,952$

Rumors at Rumor Junior High—page 28

$8:30 - 1$
$8:40 - 1 + 2 = 3$
$8:50 - 1 + 2 + 4 = 7$
$9:00 - 1 + 2 + 4 + 8 = 15$
$9:10 - 1 + 2 + 4 + 8 + 16 = 31$
$9:20 - 1 + 2 + 4 + 8 + 16 + 32 = 63$
$9:30 - 1 + 2 + 4 + 8 + 16 + 32 + 64 = 127$
$9:40 - 1 + 2 + 4 + 8 + 16 + 32 + 64 + 128 = 255$
$9:50 - 1 + 2 + 4 + 8 + 16 + 32 + 64 + 128 + 256 = 511$

4,095 students will know the rumor at 10:20.

ANSWER KEY

Count the Overlapping Triangles—page 29

Here is
one solution:

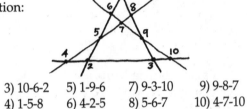

1) 1-2-3	3) 10-6-2	5) 1-9-6	7) 9-3-10	9) 9-8-7
2) 4-8-3	4) 1-5-8	6) 4-2-5	8) 5-6-7	10) 4-7-10

The Wicked King and His Plant—page 30

Fill the 5-cup container. Pour 3 cups into the 3-cup container. Empty the 3-cup container. Pour the 2 cups left in the 5-cup container into the 3-cup container. Fill the 5-cup container and pour 1 cup into the 3-cup container to fill it. Now 4 cups will be left in the 5-cup container.

The Letter M
page 31

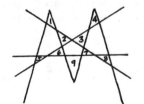

Water Wonders—page 32

Fill the 10-cup container and pour it into the 3-cup container. Pour the 3-cup container into the 7-cup container. Again fill the 3-cup container from the 10-cup and pour those 3 cups from the 3-cup container into the 7-cup container. Now there are 4 cups in the 10-cup container and 6 cups in the 7-cup container. Pour 3 of the 4 cups left in the 10-cup container into the 3-cup container. Pour 1 cup from the 3-cup container to the top of the 7-cup container. Now there is 1 cup left in the 10-cup container, 2 cups left in the 3-cup container, and the 7-cup container is full. Pour the full 7-cup container into the 10-cup container. Pour the 2 cups in the 3-cup container into the now empty 7-cup container. Now there are 8 cups in the 10-cup container and 2 cups in the 7-cup container. Finally, fill the 3-cup container from the 10-cup container and you will have 5 cups left in the 10-cup container.

ANSWER KEY

The Circle Puzzle—page 33

As many as 22 pieces can be made. Each line must cut every other line. The general equation for the number of pieces is $\dfrac{n(n+1)}{2} + 1$

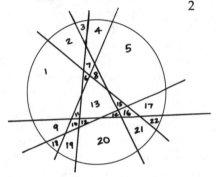

The Underground Inspector—page 34

Travel from one node to another following the path.

2-1-4-7-4-5-6-9-6-3-2-5-8-11-12-9-8-7-10-1

He will need to travel only 19 miles if he starts at node 2.

"Mom, I Need a Bike!"—page 35

$$3(6 + x) = 26 + x$$
$$18 + 3x = 26 + x$$
$$2x = 8$$
$$x = 4 \qquad \text{Her age will be } 6 + 4 = 10.$$

Don't Buy Those Motorcycles!—page 36

The young man lost 20% on the expensive one, so he got 80% of the original cost back: $600 \div .80 = 750$. Thus, the expensive one cost $750.00.

The young man made 20% on the other one, so he got 120% of the original cost back: $600 \div 1.20 = 500$.

Original cost: $750 + 500 = 1,250$

Amount received: $600 + 600 = 1,200$

Therefore, he lost $50.00 overall.

How Old Was Mrs. Johnson?—page 37

x = age of man at marriage
y = age of wife at marriage

$$x = 3y$$
$$x + 18 = 2(y + 18)$$
$$3y + 18 = 2y + 36$$
$$y = 18$$

ANSWER KEY

Patterns with Meaning—page 38

1. 26 letters in the alphabet
2. 12 months in a year
3. 4 quarts in a gallon
4. 36 black keys on a piano
5. Friday the 13th
6. the 12 days of Christmas
7. 7 wonders of the world
8. King Henry the 8th
9. The 10 Commandments
10. *Snow White and the Seven Dwarfs*
11. 9 players on a baseball team
12. The 3 wise men
13. 366 days in a leap year
14. 2,000 pounds in one ton
15. 40 days and nights of the Great Flood
16. 13 stripes on the American flag
17. 13 in a baker's dozen
18. *1,001 Arabian Nights*
19. 100 years in a century
20. 60 seconds in a minute
21. The 100 Years War
22. 101 Dalmations
23. 3 periods in a hockey game
24. 18 holes on a golf course
25. 50 states in the United States
26. 24 hours in a day

Gender Guess—page 39

For two children, there are four possible outcomes: B-B, B-G, G-B, G-G. Since B-B is ruled out, the probability of two girls is 1/3.

For the second case, G-B and G-G have been eliminated. So, the chances of two boys is 1/2.

ANSWER KEY

What's the Number?—page 40

Let x be our number. Then:

$\dfrac{x-5}{5}$ is a whole number so $\dfrac{x}{5}$ is a whole number

$\dfrac{x-6}{6}$ is a whole number so $\dfrac{x}{6}$ is a whole number

$\dfrac{x-7}{7}$ is a whole number so $\dfrac{x}{7}$ is a whole number

Because of this, x must be divisible by 5, 6, and 7! The least common multiple of 5, 6, and 7 is $5 \cdot 6 \cdot 7 = 210$.

Diffy—page 41

This game will always come to all zeros in seven levels. To improve your game, select your first four numbers randomly. That is, try to avoid numbers that make up a pattern, for example 1, 5, 10, and 15.

Nim—page 42

One winning strategy is to give your opponent a board with two rows of the same number of unused markers in each. You can match her moves and continue making two rows with the same number until you get to two rows of two and it is her move. If she takes two from any one row, simply take one of those remaining and force her to pick up the last one. You win! If she takes only one from any row, you take two and again she is forced to take the last marker. You win! (You can develop other winning strategies as you play the game.)

Absolutely Perfect Numbers—page 43

This activity requires a process of guess and check. Two people working together are more likely to find a number of this type. Other examples: 28,496 and 8,128.

Number Buddies—page 44

This activity is similar to the previous one. In fact, you can use your results from page 43 to help you here. Other examples of number buddies are:

| 5,020-5,564 | 6,230-6,368 | 10,744-10,856 |

In 1750, Leonard Euler found more than 60 pairs of buddies!

ANSWER KEY

Triangle Numbers—page 45

The pattern is 3, 6, 10, 15, 21, 28, 36, 45, 55 . . .

Wet Paint!—page 46

The longest pattern is:

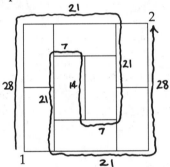

Its length is 168 units.

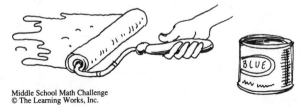

First Nine Counting Numbers—page 47

$$6 \div 3 = 2$$
$$\times$$
$$9 - 5 = 4$$
$$=$$
$$1 + 7 = 8$$

Triangle Numbers II—page 48

The pattern is 4, 9, 16, 25, 36, 49, 64, 81, 100. . .

Squares on a Table—page 49

	8	
1		7
3	2	6
4	5	

5	4	
6	1	3
7		2
8		

8		1
7	2	3
6	5	4

ANSWER KEY

How Many Ways?—page 50
12 ways.

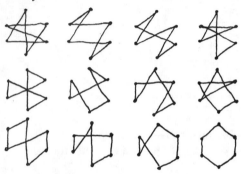

Pretty Numbers—page 51
Try the number 97.

Plus or Minus—page 52
$123 - 45 - 67 + 89 = 100$

Every Wall Has a Door—page 53
Here is one possible solution for each puzzle. Note that puzzle (b) has no solution.

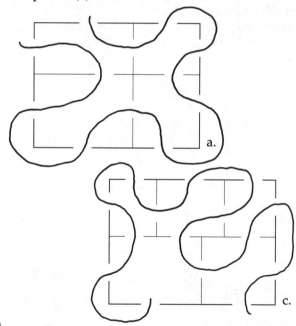

ANSWER KEY

Pluses—page 54

$9 + 8 + 7 + 65 + 4 + 3 + 2 + 1 = 99$

$1 + 2 + 34 + 56 + 7 = 100$

$1 + 23 + 4 + 5 + 67 = 100$

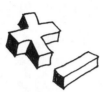

Four Fours—page 55

$4 - 4 + 4 - 4 = 0$

$(4 - 4) + (4 \div 4) = 1$

$(4 \div 4) + (4 \div 4) = 2$

$(4 + 4 + 4) \div 4 = 3$

$(4 - 4) + (\sqrt{4} + \sqrt{4}) = 4$

$(4 \div 4) + (\sqrt{4} + \sqrt{4}) = 5$

$(4 + 4 + 4) \div \sqrt{4} = 6$

$(4 + \sqrt{4}) + \frac{4}{4} = 7$

$\sqrt{4} + \sqrt{4} + \sqrt{4} + \sqrt{4} = 8$

$(4 + 4) + (4 \div 4) = 9$

$(4 \bullet 4) - (4 + \sqrt{4}) = 10$

$44 \div (\sqrt{4} + \sqrt{4}) = 11$

$(4 \bullet 4) - (\sqrt{4} + \sqrt{4}) = 12$

$\frac{44}{4} + \sqrt{4} = 13$

$(4 \bullet 4) - 4 + \sqrt{4} = 14$

$(4 \bullet 4) - \frac{4}{4} = 15$

$4 + 4 + 4 + 4 = 16$

$(4 \bullet 4) + \frac{4}{4} = 17$

$(4 \bullet 4) + 4 - \sqrt{4} = 18$

$4! - 4 - \frac{4}{4} = 19$

$4! + 4 - 4 - 4 = 20$

$(4! - 4) + \frac{4}{4} = 21$

$\frac{44}{4} \bullet \sqrt{4} = 22$

$(4! + \frac{4}{4}) - \sqrt{4} = 23$

$(4! + 4) - \sqrt{4} - \sqrt{4} = 24$

$(4! + \sqrt{4}) - \frac{4}{4} = 25$

$(4! + \sqrt{4}) + 4 - 4 = 26$

$(4! + 4) - \frac{4}{4} = 27$

$(4! + 4) - \sqrt{4} + \sqrt{4} = 28$

$(4! + \frac{4}{4}) + 4 = 29$

$(\sqrt{4} \bullet 4 \bullet 4) - \sqrt{4} = 30$

$4! + \sqrt{4} \div .4 + \sqrt{4} = 31$

$(4 \bullet 4) + (4 \bullet 4) = 32$

$4! + \sqrt{4} \div .4 + 4 = 33$

$4! + 4 + 4 + \sqrt{4} = 34$

$4! + \frac{44}{4} = 35$

$4! + 4 + 4 + 4 = 36$

$(4! + \sqrt{4}) \div \sqrt{4} + 4! = 37$

$44 - 4 - \sqrt{4} = 38$

$44 - \sqrt{4} \div .4 = 39$

$4! + 4! - 4 - 4 = 40$

$4 \bullet 4 + .4 \div .4 = 41$

$4! + 4! - 4 - \sqrt{4} = 42$

$44 - \frac{4}{4} = 43$

$4! + 4! - \sqrt{4} - \sqrt{4} = 44$

$44 + \frac{4}{4} = 45$

$4! + 4! - 4 + \sqrt{4} = 46$

$4! + 4! - \frac{4}{4} = 47$

$4! + 4! + 4! - 4! = 48$

$4! + 4! + \frac{4}{4} = 49$

ANSWER KEY

It Makes One Hundred—page 56

$(5 - (5 \div 5)) \bullet (5 \bullet 5) = 100$

$(5 \bullet 5 \bullet 5) - (5 \bullet 5) = 100$

A Magic Triangle—page 57

```
      1                  1
    9 /\ 6             7 /\ 5
   4 /__\ 8           6 /__\ 9
  3   7  5  2        3   4  8  2
```

The First 19 Numbers—page 58

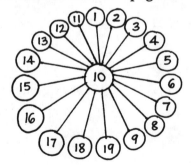

The Clock Face—page 59

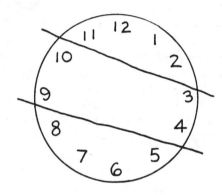

Bridges—page 60

Each player needs to both block and move forward. Starting more than one possible path is a good strategy.

ANSWER KEY

The Even Number Wins—page 61

The first player takes two clips and then:

1. If the second player takes an even number of clips, you leave him or her an amount that is 1 larger than a multiple of 6 (e.g., 19, 13, 7, etc.).
2. If the second player takes an odd number of clips, you leave him or her a number that is smaller by 1 than a multiple of 6 (e.g., 23, 17, 11, 5). If this is impossible, leave a number that is a multiple of 6 (e.g., 24, 18, 12, 6). For example, you take 2 and your opponent takes 3 leaving 22. You can't take 5 to leave 17, so take 4 leaving 18.

Boxes—page 62

If you want to add an interesting twist to this game, use the rule that after a player's boxes have been added up, the player may increase her score by the area of all rectangles she has whose sides are both larger than one unit. For example, if a player has this rectangle

she can increase her score by 6. (3 x 2 = 6)

My Dad and I—page 63

Let x be the number of years since my dad was 31. So, today we get

$$(31 + x) = 2(8 + x)$$
$$31 + x = 16 + 2x$$
$$15 = x$$

Therefore, my dad's age today is: $31 + x = 46$, and my age is: $8 + x = 23$.

Five Gold Chains—page 64

The correct answer is $4.50. Take one group of three and break each one. This will cost $1.50. Now, use each of these to join two of the other groups. This will cost $3.00.

ANSWER KEY

Mail on the Luxury Liner—page 65

Let x = speed of luxury liner
10x = speed of helicopter
Distance of helicopter = 10x • (time to reach liner)
Distance of liner = x • (time) + 360

Since the distance the liner will travel after the helicopter takes off after it is d = x • t, and we know:

$$10x • t = x • t + 360$$
$$10d = d + 360$$
$$9d = 360$$
$$d = 40$$

then the distance the liner will travel in total will be 40 + 360 = 400 miles.

The Seven Bulldogs—page 66

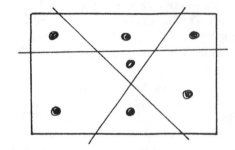

Eleven Separate Enclosures—page 67

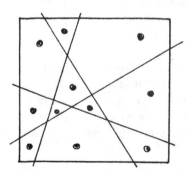

ANSWER KEY

A Topsy Turvy Year—page 68
Try 1961.

Division—page 69
Subtract each number from every other. We get 895; 1,253; 1,611; 716; 358; and 358. Notice that 358 came up twice and that $358 = 2 \cdot 179$. Thus, the only number that can divide in every case with no remainder is 179. So 179 is the divisor we want. By checking, one sees that it will always leave a remainder of 164.

Proof That 1 + 1 = 3—page 70
The problem is with the step where one divides by $(x + y - 3)$ because $x + y - 3 = 0$, and you can't divide by zero!

Stack It Again, Sam!—page 71
The paper stack will be over 88 million miles high!

Cubes from Squares—page 72
Here are several solutions. There are others.

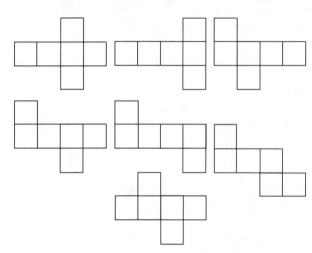

Weird Number Patterns—page 73
This activity allows students to discover some interesting number patterns.

ANSWER KEY

Howlers—page 74

The solution lies in the fraction $\dfrac{10x + a}{10a + y} = \dfrac{x}{y}$

If we solve it, we see $y = \dfrac{10ax}{9x + a}$ must be an integer.

So we can try various numbers for a and x and see if our result is an integer.

Letters for Digits—page 75

$$
\begin{array}{r}
9{,}108 \\
-\,1{,}089 \\
\hline
8{,}019
\end{array}
$$

The Diamond Ring—page 76

The diamond ring costs $300.

Two Pages in a Book—page 77

The pages are 25 and 26.

Playing With Sugar Cubes—page 78

The correct number is 64.

More Addition—page 79

The answer is 210.

Prime Years—page 80

1951, 1973, 1979, 1987, 1993, and 1997

Paper Strips—page 81

76 square inches

Inscribed Angles—page 82

90 degrees each

A Sequence of Numbers—page 83

400

 (mirror images of the numbers 1–7)

50

128

127

8

333

36

ANSWER KEY

The First Six Non-Zero Digits—page 84

$$\begin{array}{r} 54 \\ \times\ 3 \\ \hline 162 \end{array}$$

A Fibonacci Surprise—page 85

Let a and b represent the first two terms of the sequence from where you start. In general then you will get

a, b, a + b, a + 2b, 2a + 3b, 3a + 5b, 5a + 8b, 8a + 13b, 13a + 21b, 21a + 34b

When you add these 10 terms, you get 55a + 88b = 11(5a + 8b) and 5a + 8b is the seventh term of our general sequence.

Aristotle's Wheel—page 86

Galileo analyzed it from the point of view of two concentric squares (i.e., square wheels). He notes

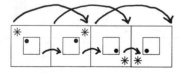

that the small inside square traced itself out, but the corners made three jumps. You can argue this approach with a five-sided wheel, a six-sided wheel, a 10-sided wheel, a wheel with any number of sides. A circle could be thought of as an infinite sided regular polygon. In this case, in place of three or four or nine jumps you would have an infinite number of infinitely small jumps. This accounts for the distance not traveled.

Twin Primes—page 88

They are 11-13, 17-19, 29-31, 41-43, 59-61, and 71-73.

The Sieve of Eratosthenes—page 90

There are 25 primes.

Connect the Shapes—page 91

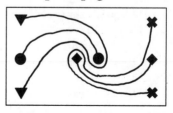

ANSWER KEY

A Five-Digit Number—page 92

For 12R3T to be divisible by 4, 3T must be 32 or 36. For 12R3T to be divisible by 9, 1 +2 + R + 3 + T must be an even multiple of 9. If T is 2, R must be 1. If T is 6, R must be 6. So T must be 2 and R must be 1.

Making Change—page 93

14 in all. 2 Pennies (P); 2 Nickels (N); 1 Dime (D)

1P			=	1 cent
2P			=	2 cents
1P	1N		=	6 cents
1P	2N		=	11 cents
2P	1N		=	7 cents
2P	2N		=	12 cents
1P	1N	1D	=	16 cents
2P	1N	1D	=	17 cents
1P	2N	1D	=	21 cents
2P	2N	1D	=	22 cents
	1N		=	5 cents
	2N	1D	=	20 cents
	1N	1D	=	15 cents
		1D	=	10 cents

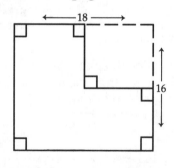

The Magic Square—page 94

$$11 + S + 14 = S + R + W$$
$$25 = R + W$$
$$V + W + 19 = 14 + R + V$$
$$W = R - 5$$
$$\text{So,} \quad 25 = R + (R - 5)$$
$$30 = 2R$$
$$\mathbf{15 = R}$$

Find the Perimeter—page 95

$$16 + 18 + 16 + 18 = 68$$

ANSWER KEY

It's the Product—page 96

We can see that 2 • R must end in 6. So R must be 8 or 3. If R is 3, the numbers will be too small. So R must be 8.

Bikes and Trikes—page 97

Solution 1:

Let x = number of bicycles
and y = number of tricycles.
Number of items: $x + y = 7$
Number of wheels: $2x + 3y = 19$
$$y = 7 - x \quad 2x + 3(7 - x) = 19$$
$$2x + 21 - 3x = 19$$
$$-x = -2$$
$$x = 2 \text{ bicycles}$$
$$y = 5 \text{ tricycles}$$

Solution 2:

If all the items made were bicycles, we would have 14 wheels used. That would leave 5. Now match these 5 single wheels with one pair each in the 7 pairs. You get 5 tricycles and 2 bicycles.

One Billion Dollars—page 98

Silver will always weigh more!

A Quarter—page 99

Twelve in all. Pennies (P); Nickels (N); Dimes (D)

one type	two types	three types
25P	20P 1N	5P 2N 1D
5N	15P 2N	15P 1N 1D
	10P 3N	
	5P 4N	
	15P 1D	
	3N 1D	
	1N 2D	
	5P 2D	

Candy Bars—page 100

Let x be the first child's number.
Let y be the second child's number.
$x + 1 = y - 1$ so $y = 2 + x$
also $2(x - 1) = y + 1$. Now substitute and get
$$2(x - 1) = (2 + x) + 1$$
$$2x - 2 = x + 3$$
so $x = 5$ and $y = 7$

ANSWER KEY

Jogging Shoes—page 101

She will need to take out at least 11 shoes.

Count Your Diagonals—page 102

Six diagonals: 20 octagon

14 heptagon   20 − 14 = 6

The Planet Zot—page 103

"Zut-zut-zut-zut."

A Fifty Cent Piece—page 104

Forty-nine ways. (Q) Quarters

one type	two types	two types
50P	6N 2D	40P 2N
10N	4N 3D	35P 3N
5D	2N 4D	30P 4N
2Q	40P 1D	25P 5N
two types	30P 2D	20P 6N
5N 1Q	20P 3D	15P 7N
25P 1Q	10P 4D	10P 8N
8N 1D	45P 1N	5P 9N

three types	three types	four types
35P 1N 1D	15P 1N 3D	10P 1N 1D 1Q
30P 2N 1D	10P 2N 3D	5P 2N 1D 1Q
25P 3N 1D	5P 3N 3D	
20P 4N 1D	5P 1N 4D	
15P 5N 1D	5P 2D 1Q	
10P 6N 1D	15P 1D 1Q	
5P 7N 1D	1N 2D 1Q	
25P 1N 2D	3N 1D 1Q	
20P 2N 2D	5P 4N 1Q	
15P 3N 2D	10P 3N 1Q	
10P 4N 2D	15P 2N 1Q	
5P 5N 2D	20P 1N 1Q	

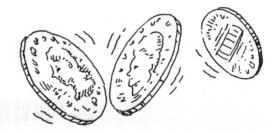

ANSWER KEY

Big Money—page 105

The answer is 3. One way of solving this problem is to make a list of multiples of 8 with seven added to them and then do the same with multiples of 6 with 3 added on, and finally do the same with multiples of 5 with 4 added on, and then match the lists.

$8 + 7 = 15$	$6 + 3 = 9$	$5 + 4 = 9$
$16 + 7 = 23$	$12 + 3 = 15$	$10 + 4 = 14$
$24 + 7 = 31$	$18 + 3 = 21$	$15 + 4 = 19$
$32 + 7 = \underline{39}$	$24 + 3 = 27$	$20 + 4 = 24$
$40 + 7 = 47$	$30 + 3 = 33$	$25 + 4 = 29$
$48 + 7 = 55$	$36 + 3 = \underline{39}$	$30 + 4 = 34$
$56 + 7 = 63$	$42 + 3 = 45$	$35 + 4 = \underline{39}$

This gives us 39 and

$$\begin{array}{r} 4\ R\ 3 \\ 9\overline{)\,39} \\ \underline{36} \\ 3 \end{array} \quad \text{(3 left over)}$$

A Number Pyramid—page 106

149. The student can write down the pattern of the first element in each level. Then he or she will find that you simply add successive odd numbers:

```
1  2   5  10  17  26  37  50  65  82  101 122 145
 \/ \/ \/ \/ \/  \/  \/  \/  \/  \/  \/  \/
 1  3   5   7   9  11  13  15  17  19  21  23
```

So 145 is the first item in level 13. The fifth is 149.

Don't Lift Your Pen!—page 107

Here is one solution:

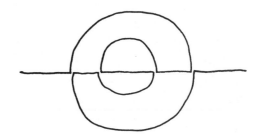

ANSWER KEY

House Building—page 108
Thirty-six.

The 12 apprentices can build 12 houses in 12 days.
12 carpenters can build 12 houses in 6 days. So
they can build 24 houses in 12 days. $12 + 24 = 36$.

How Many Triangles?—page 109
Forty-one. $16 + 8 + 8 + 2 + 2 + 1 + 1 + 1 + 1 + 1 = 41$.

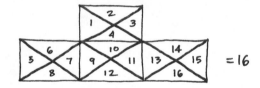

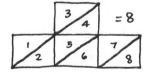

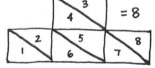

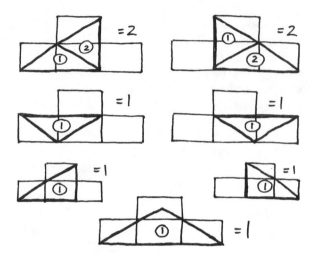

Tip Top—page 110
Playing this game gives students practice in
division and multiplication.

Diffy

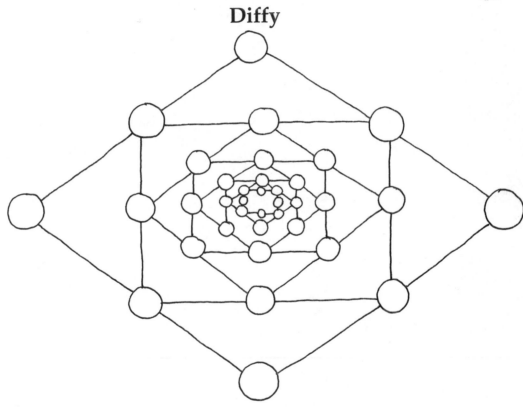

Bridges

Boxes

A Note to Students

The problems in this book are meant to be open-ended. The answers provided in the answer key are, in many cases, not the only solutions. Likewise, there is more than one way to solve each problem. Have fun coming up with your own creative ways to solve these problems.